In The Potter's Hands

Robert Eimer, O.M.I., & Sarah O'Malley, O.S.B.

Resource Publications, Inc.
160 E. Virginia St. #290
San Jose, CA 95112

+ Most Rev. Thomas J. O'Brien
Bishop of Phoenix, Arizona
May 7, 1988

Editorial director: Kenneth Guentert
Production editor: Elizabeth J. Asborno
Cover design and production: Ron Niewald and Andrew Wong
Cover and inside illustrations: Michele Stapely

Library of Congress Cataloging in Publication Data:

O'Malley, Sarah.   In the potter's hands.

1. Wake services—Texts. 2. Catholic Church—
Liturgy—Texts. I. Eimer, Robert, 1927-
BX2045.W34054   1988   265'.85   88-24017
ISBN 0-89390-132-6

5 4 3 2 1

To John Foley, Fred Olson, and Bruce Lobermeier for their sensitive service to the people of the West End, Duluth, Minnesota.

Contents

Introduction 1

ADVENT/CHRISTMAS
Like Incense Before You 5
God of Faithfulness 12
LENT
Life Is Changed, Not Ended 19
The Cross Is Our Salvation 25
EASTER/PENTECOST
Birth Unto Hope 32
Light That Conquers Darkness 39
ORDINARY TIME
Food for the Journey 46
In the Potter's Hands 53
The Life-Giving Word of God 60

Appendix 1: Alternate Scripture Readings 67
Appendix 2: Music for Wake Services 68

Introduction

One of the first ritual revisions to take place after the Second Vatican Council was the issuance of a new rite of funerals. After many years of use, the new rite was reviewed. Subsequently, the U.S. bishops submitted a new order of Christian funerals for approval by Rome. That new order should be issued in the near future. Although *The Order of Christian Funerals* awaits confirmation, the document has already stimulated much discussion in liturgical workshops around the country. Varied commentaries on the document are already beginning to appear.

The Order of Christian Funerals offers many challenges and options to planners and celebrants of funeral rites. By providing broader choices, greater personalization, and flexibility, it permits a richer adaptation to the Church's ministry to the bereaved. This booklet, *In The Potter's Hands*, provides nine wake services based on the spirit and guidelines approved by the U.S. bishops in 1985.

The Order of Christian Funerals divides the funeral into six rites. Without going into detail about each of the six rites, we should note that the document reaffirms the value of the fourth rite — the Vigil or Wake service, whether it is celebrated at the home, in the church, or at the mortuary. The document calls the wake service the principal rite between the death and the funeral liturgy.

For many years in Catholic wake services, the rosary has, with few exceptions, been the preferred prayer form. But since Vatican II, ordained ministers have begun to use Bible-centered wake services, especially when the gathered family and friends come from various Christian denominations. Unfortunately, the number and variety of scriptural wake services available on the market have been meager.

Our purpose in composing these nine wake services is fourfold:

1) to provide vigil services according to the scriptural spirit found in *The Order of Christian Funerals* (nos. 56 & 59). The proclaiming of God's word is at the very heart of Christian ritual. *In The Potter's Hands* is scripturally inspired, depending heavily on praying the psalms and reading passages from both Old and New Testaments;

2) to emphasize the wake service as a time to support people in their grief and to bring hope and consolation to the bereaved through prayer and Christian presence. *The Order of Christian Funerals* (no. 56) envisions the wake service as a time when Christ, present in the community, consoles and strengthens the family of the bereaved. The psalms used in each of our wake services follow a simple pattern: the first psalm expresses grief while the second psalm assures the bereaved that God's love and help are present. In the spirit of *The Order of Christian Funerals* (no. 62), we recommend a time of personal sharing by family or friends at the end of the service. The intimate sharing of personal tributes and stories is more suited to the wake service than to the Eucharistic Celebration proper;

3) to create a variety of vigil services that also reflect the liturgical seasons of the Church. Following the liturgical year, the nine wake services are arranged as follows: two for

Advent/Christmas, two for Lent, two for Easter/Pentecost, and three for Ordinary Time. However, this is only a suggested listing. Services proper to one season could reasonably be adapted to other times/seasons. More importantly, nine wake services will allow the family and the minister to make some personal choices;

4) to unify each service around a symbol and a theme. In doing this, we have researched scriptural readings and prayers that are appropriate to each theme and symbol. Likewise, we used the simplest of symbols, nearly all of which are found in the funeral liturgy itself — incense, the cross, flowers, water, a candle, a Bible, an earthen vase, bread and wine, and an evergreen branch. By choosing these symbols, we hoped they would be readily accessible to busy ministers. The local mortuary might also keep most of these symbols available. We intended that the use of these symbols in a wake service might reinforce and deepen their meaning when experienced in the funeral liturgy proper. The use of familiar symbols at the wake might also be of great benefit to those unable to be present at the funeral rites.

In the Potter's Hands is not meant to be an exclusively Catholic booklet. We believe that the symbols and themes are universal in Christianity and that all denominations would feel comfortable with our scripture-centered wake services.

This booklet was not designed for ordained clergy only (priests, deacons, and Protestant ministers). In the light of the continuing clergy shortage, more and more wake services will of necessity be conducted by religious or lay bereavement ministers. *In the Potter's Hands* contains a variety of wake services that are a valuable resource to any leader of ritual, ordained or not. In light of the above, we did not use the term "clergy" for the presider; we opted for the term "minister."

Additional scripture references listed in the appendix offer still greater variety for the minister who would prefer to choose other readings.

A few comments about the structure of the wake service. Basically, it is a minimal adaptation of the office of the dead, with the psalms first and the liturgy of the word following. Nothing prevents the presider from making an adaptation of the service — namely, placing the psalms as responses to the readings. Secondly, we recommend two Scripture readings. The first reading allows a choice between an Old Testament or New Testament reading (readings A or B). The second reading is taken from the Gospels. Nothing prohibits the leader from using all three readings.

The liturgical music found in the appendix was selected for its familiarity and appropriateness to the vigil service. *The Order of Christian Funerals* strongly urges the use of well-chosen music both in the vigil and the funeral liturgy proper (no. 68).

We thank Fr. John Gallen, S.J., and Fr. Ron Brassard for their comments and suggestions. Likewise, we thank Michele Stapley for the cover design and artwork.

We also want to thank the following Phoenix, AZ, funeral directors whom we consulted: Dave Shumway, Edward Murphy, Nick Lutz, Tom Carrick. They were of great help in offering suggestions.

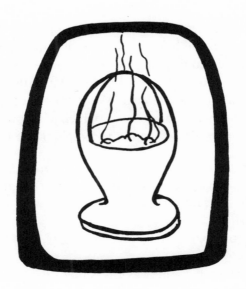

Like Incense Before You

Symbol: Incense
Suggested Season: Advent/Christmas or Ordinary Time

Introduction
Remain seated during the service till the Gospel.

OPENING SONG

WELCOME/INTRODUCTION OF THEME
The minister welcomes the family and friends informally and then proceeds with the service by making the sign of the cross and introducing the theme of the wake service (the minister can read the following introduction or comment on the symbol in his/her own words:)

Minister: Incense was an important part of Jewish worship. In the psalms and in the book of Revelation, incense represents the prayer of the people rising to God. Incense also was a sign of honor. Consequently, the Magi presented incense to the child Jesus as a sign of reverence. We gather as church to give honor to the body of _____, which at Baptism became a part of the Body of Christ and the temple of the Holy Spirit.

The minister should have a container of charcoal lit before the service begins. The minister or a family member may now place incense on the burning coals.

OPENING PRAYER

Minister: Heavenly Father, as the smoke of incense rises before your throne, so may our prayers for _____ rise also. Let the incense enfold the body of _____ and honor it as a member of Christ's body and a worthy temple of the Holy Spirit. Grant this prayer through the intercession of your Son. Amen.

Liturgy of the Word

PSALMS
The psalms may be recited by the gathering as a whole or alternately by sides 1 and 2.

● Psalm 141, 1-4a, 8-9_____

All: To you, **O LORD, I call.**

Side 1:
O LORD, to you I call; hasten to me;
  hearken to my voice when I call upon you.
Let my prayer come like incense before you;
  the lifting up of my hands, like the evening sacrifice.

Side 2:
O LORD, set a watch before my mouth,
  a guard at the door of my lips.
Let not my heart incline to the evil
  of engaging in deeds of wickedness.

Side 1:
For toward you, O GOD, my LORD, my eyes are turned;
  in you I take refuge; strip me not of life.
Keep me from the trap they have set for me.

● Psalm 116, 12-19 _____

All: Precious in the eyes of the LORD is the death of his
faithful ones.

Side 1:
How shall I make a return to the LORD
  for all the good he has done for me?
The cup of salvation I will take up,
  and I will call upon the name of the LORD.

Side 2:
My vows to the LORD I will pay
  in the presence of all his people.
Precious in the eyes of the LORD
  is the death of his faithful ones.

Side 1:
O LORD, I am your servant;
  I am your servant, the son of your handmaid;
  you have loosed my bonds.
To you will I offer sacrifice of thanksgiving
  and I will call upon the name of the LORD.

Side 2:
My vows to the LORD I will pay
  in the presence of all his people.
In the courts of the house of the LORD,
  in your midst, O Jerusalem.

SCRIPTURE READINGS
A member or friend of the family may present Reading A or B.

● Reading A _____

Reader: A reading from the book of Exodus (30, 34-38)

Yahweh said to Moses, "Take sweet spices: storax, onycha, galbanum, sweet spices and pure frankincense in equal parts, and compound and incense, such a blend as the perfumer might make, salted, pure, and holy. Crush a part of it into a fine powder, and put some of this in front of the Testimony in the Tent of Meeting, the place appointed for my meetings with you. You must regard it as most holy. You are not to make any incense of similar composition for your own use. You must hold it to be a holy thing, reserved for Yahweh. Whoever copies it for use as a perfume shall be outlawed from his people."

This is the Word of the Lord.

● Reading B _____

Reader: A reading from Revelation 8, (2-5)

Next I saw seven trumpets being given to the seven angels who stand in the presence of God. Another angel, who had a golden censer, came and stood at the altar. A large quantity of incense was given to him to offer with the prayers of all the saints on the golden altar that stood in front of the throne; and so from the angel's hand the smoke of the incense went up in the presence of God and with it the prayers of the saints.

This is the Word of the Lord.

Silence is suggested after the first reading. The Alleluia or another appropriate verse or song may introduce the Gospel.

● Gospel reading _____

(Stand)

Minister: A reading from the Gospel according to Matthew
(2, 1-4, 7-12.

After Jesus had been born at Bethlehem in Judaea during the
reign of King Herod, some wise men came to Jerusalem from
the east. "Where is the infant king of the Jews?" they asked.
"We saw his star as it rose and have come to do him
homage." When King Herod heard this he was perturbed,
and so was the whole of Jerusalem. He called together all the
chief priests and the scribes of the people. Then Herod
summoned the wise men to see him privately. He asked them
the exact date on which the star had appeared, and sent them
on to Bethlehem. "Go and find out all about the child," he
said, "and when you have found him, let me know, so that I
too may go and do him homage." Having listened to what the
king had to say, they set out. And there in front of them was
the star they had seen rising: it went forward and halted over
the place where the child was. The sight of the star filled them
with delight, and going into the house they saw the child with
his mother Mary, and falling to their knees they did him
homage. Then opening their treasures, they offered him gifts
of gold and frankincense and myrrh. But they were warned in
a dream not to go back to Herod, and returned to their own
country by a different way.

This is the Gospel of the Lord.

(Sit)

Homily
A brief homily based on the readings may be given.

Prayers of Intercession

LITANY

Minister: Friends, let us join together in prayer:

Heavenly Father, may the faith, hope, and love of your family rise up to you like incense.

All: **Our prayer, like incense, rises.**

Minister: May the smoke of incense, Lord, surround the body of _____ and make that body sacred in your sight.

All: **Our prayer, like incense, rises.**

Minister: May the goodness of _____'s life smell like perfume, O Lord, and make him/her pleasing to you.

All: **Our prayer, like incense, rises.**

Minister: Jesus, you received frankincense as a gift at your birth. May our prayers accompany _____ in his/her new birth into eternal life.

All: **Our prayer, like incense, rises.**

LORD'S PRAYER

Minister: Father, let this prayer come before you like incense, as we say, "Our Father..."

CONCLUDING PRAYER

Minister: Father, we ask that you raise _____ on the last day and welcome him/her to your heavenly mansion. Like incense, may the prayers of your sons and daughters intercede for _____, who journeyed through this world and passed on to the next.

All: **Amen.**

It would be an appropriate time for members of the family or for friends to share their memories of the deceased. Likewise it would be a suitable time to share a poem or letter or to comment on a keepsake or simply to reminisce.

Concluding Rite

BLESSING OF THE BODY
The assembly is invited to bow their heads as the minister prays the final blessing:

Minister: We give you praise and we thank you, Father, for you formed our bodies from the dust of your beautiful creation, breathed into us your spirit, and gave us delight that we can see, smell and hear, that we can taste and touch. We praise you, Lord, for _____, whose body was a temple of your spirit, and we bless his/her body as we await the resurrection of the dead and the life of the world to come.

All: **Amen.**

A suitable song may conclude the service.

God of Faithfulness

Symbol: Evergreen branch/wreath
Suggested Season: Advent/Christmas or Ordinary Time

Introduction
Remain seated during the service till the Gospel.

OPENING SONG

WELCOME/INTRODUCTION OF THEME
The minister welcomes the family and friends informally and then proceeds with the service by making the sign of the cross and introducing the theme of the wake service (the minister can read the following or comment on the symbol in his/her own words:)

Minister: The evergreen is a symbol of faithfulness for it remains green even when other plants seem dead and drab. Like the evergreen, God is faithful to the promises he has made to us in the Scriptures: promises of friendship, forgiveness, and eternal life.

The minister or one of the family now places the evergreen branch or wreath on or near the casket.

OPENING PRAYER

Minister: God our Father, as your children, in this time of sorrow we rely on your faithfulness to your promise of eternal life. Bring _____ to your heavenly mansion, which you have reserved for him/her for all eternity. Amen.

Liturgy of the Word

PSALMS
The psalms may be recited by the gathering as a whole or alternately by sides 1 and 2.

• Psalm 130, 1-6 _____

All: **Out of the depths I cry to you, O LORD.**

Side 1:
Out of the depths I cry to you, O LORD;
  LORD, hear my voice!
Let your ears be attentive
  to my voice in supplication:

Side 2:
If you, O LORD, mark iniquities,
  LORD, who can stand?
But with you is forgiveness,
  that you may be revered.

Side 1:
I trust in the LORD:
  my soul trusts in his word.

Side 2:
My soul waits for the LORD
  more than sentinels wait for the dawn.

● Psalm 100, 1-5 _____

All: The LORD, whose, kindness endures forever.

Side 1:
Sing joyfully to the LORD, all you lands:
  serve the LORD with gladness
  come before him with joyful song.

Side 2:
Know that the LORD is God;
  he made us, his we are:
  his people, the flock he tends.
Enter his gates with thanksgiving,
  his courts with praise;

Side 1:
Give thanks to him; bless his name for he is good;
the LORD, whose kindness endures forever,
  and his faithfulness, to all generations.

SCRIPTURE READINGS
A member or friend of the family may present Reading A or B.

● Reading A _____

Reader: A reading from the Book of Lamentations (3, 22-26)

The favors of Yahweh are not all past,
  his kindnesses are not exhausted;
every morning they are renewed;
  great is his faithfulness.
"My portion is Yahweh" says my soul
  "and so I will hope in him."

Yahweh is good to those who trust him,
  to the soul that searches for him.
It is good to wait in silence
  for Yahweh to save.

This is the Word of the Lord.

● Reading B _____

Reader: A reading from the second letter to Timothy (2, 11-13)

Here is a saying that you can rely on:

If we have died with him, then we shall live with him.
If we hold firm, then we shall reign with him.
If we disown him, then he will disown us.
We may be unfaithful, but he is always faithful,
for he cannot disown his own self.

This is the Word of the Lord.

Silence is suggested after the first reading. The Alleluia or another appropriate verse or song may introduce the Gospel.

● Gospel Reading _____

(Stand)

Reader: A reading from the Gospel according to John (10, 14-18)

I am the good shepherd;
I know my own
and my own know me,
just as the Father knows me
and I know the Father;
and I lay down my life for my sheep.
And there are other sheep I have
that are not of this fold,
and these I have to lead as well.
They too will listen to my voice,
and there will be only one flock,
and one shepherd.

The Father loves me,
because I lay down my life
in order to take it up again.
No one takes it from me;
I lay it down of my own free will,
and as it is in my power to lay it down,
so it is in my power to take it up again:
and this is the command I have been given by my Father."

This is the Gospel of the Lord.

(Sit)

Homily

A brief homily based on the readings may be given.

Prayers of Intercession

LITANY

Minister: Lord Jesus, mindful of your ever-faithful love for your people, we come to you in great confidence as we pray:

God of faithfulness, look kindly on your friend _____.
Grant him/her an everlasting home with you. We pray...

All: **Remember us, O Lord.**

Minister: Jesus, true to your promise of a share in the eternal banquet, grant peace and strength to us who feel the pain of separation. We pray...

All: **Remember us, O Lord.**

Minister: Spirit of consolation, in our loss we turn to you for comfort. Enable us then to comfort one another. We pray...

All: **Remember us, O Lord.**

Minister: You are a God of mystery. May we who struggle with the mystery of life and death be heartened by your promise of eternal life. We pray...

All: **Remember us, O Lord.**

Minister: As we remember _____, who in life followed you, keep us faithful in your service and strengthen us on our pilgrimage through life. We pray...

All: **Remember us, O Lord.**

Minister: Model of faithful love, bring us all together in that kingdom where love reigns. We pray...

All: **Remember us, O Lord.**

LORD'S PRAYER

Minister: Confident that God our Father will remain faithful to his children, we say **"Our Father..."**

CONCLUDING PRAYER

Minister: Let us pray.

God, ever-faithful to your promises, we trust that You have heard our prayers. In your goodness bring us all together again one day in our eternal home. We ask this through Christ our Lord.

All: **Amen.**

It would be an appropriate time for members of the family and for friends to share their memories of the deceased. It would also be a suitable time to share a poem or letter or to comment on a keepsake or simply to reminisce.

Concluding Rite

BLESSING OF THE BODY

The assembly is invited to bow their heads as the minister prays the final blessing:

Minister: We give you praise and we thank you, Father, for you formed our bodies from the dust of your beautiful creation, breathed into us your spirit, and gave us delight that we can see, smell and hear, that we can taste and touch. We praise you Lord, for _____, whose body was a temple of your spirit, and we bless his/her body as we await the resurrection of the dead and the life of the world to come.

All: **Amen.**

A suitable song may conclude the service.

Life Is Changed, Not Ended

Symbol: Flower
Suggested Season: Lent or Ordinary Time

Introduction
Remain seated during the service till the Gospel.

OPENING SONG *after Introduction + Opening Prayer*

WELCOME/INTRODUCTION OF THEME
The minister welcomes the family and friends informally and then proceeds with the service by making the sign of the cross and introducing the theme of the wake service (the minister can read the following introduction or comment on the symbol in his/her own words:)

Minister: The seed that blossoms into a flower is a symbol of God's new life. Our lowly bodies, buried in the earth like the seed, will blossom into a *new life*, a fuller, more beautiful life where there will be no sorrow or tears. The flower is the wondrous fulfillment of the seed. The flowers given at the time of death represent the glorious resurrected life of the deceased.

OPENING PRAYER

Minister: Heavenly Father, the seed planted in the earth brings forth the crowning glory of the flower. May the life of _____, like the seed, not be ended but rather blossom into the wondrous new life promised by Jesus, our Savior. Amen.

The minister or family member may now place a special flower or bouquet near or upon the casket.

Liturgy of the Word

PSALMS
The psalms may be recited by the gathering as a whole or alternately by sides 1 and 2.

● Psalm 22, 2-6 _____

All: My God, my God, why have you forsaken me?

Side 1:
My God, my God, why have you forsaken me?
  far from my prayer, from the words of my cry?

Side 2:
O my God, I cry out by day, and you answer not;
  by night, and there is no relief for me.
Yet you are enthroned in the holy place,
  O glory of Israel!

Side 1:

In you our fathers trusted;
  they trusted, and you delivered them.
To you they cried and they escaped,
  in you they trusted, and they were not put to shame.

● Psalm 36, 6-10 _____

All: You are the source of all life.

Side 1:

O LORD, your kindness reaches to heaven;
  your faithfulness, to the clouds.
Your justice is like the mountains of God;
  your judgments, like the mighty deep;
  man and beast you save, O LORD.

Side 2:

How precious is your kindness, O God!
  The children of men take refuge in the shadow of your wings.

Side 1:

They have their fill of the prime gifts of your house;
  from your delightful stream you give them to drink.
For with you is the fountain of life,
  and in your light we see light.

SCRIPTURE READINGS

A member or friend of the family may present Reading A or B.

● Reading A _____

Reader: A reading from the book of Genesis (1, 11-12)

God said, "Let the earth produce vegetation: seed-bearing plants, and fruit trees bearing fruit with their seed inside, on the earth." And so it was. The earth produced vegetation: plants bearing seed in their several kinds, and trees bearing fruit with their seed inside in their several kinds. God saw that it was good. Evening came and morning came: the third day. This is the Word of the Lord.

● Reading B _____

Reader: A reading from the first letter of Paul to the Corinthians (15, 35-38; 42-44)

Someone may ask, "How are dead people raised, and what sort of body do they have when they come back?" They are stupid questions. Whatever you sow in the ground has to die before it is given new life/and the thing that you sow is not what is going to come; you sow a bare grain, say of wheat or something like that, and then God gives it the sort of body that he has chosen: each sort of seed gets its own sort of body.

It is the same with the resurrection of the dead: the thing that is sown is perishable but what is raised is imperishable; the thing that is sown is contemptible but what is raised is glorious; the thing that is sown is weak but what is raised is powerful; when it is sown it embodies the soul, when it is raised it embodies the spirit."

This is the Word of the Lord.

Silence is suggested after the first reading. The Alleluia or another appropriate verse or song may introduce the Gospel.

● Gospel reading _____

(Stand)

Minister: A reading from the Gospel according to John (12, 23-25)

Jesus replied to them:

"Now the hour has come
for the Son of Man to be glorified.
I tell you, most solemnly,
unless a wheat grain falls on the ground and dies,
it remains only a single grain;
but if it dies,
it yields a rich harvest.

Anyone who loves his life loses it;
anyone who hates his life in this world
will keep it for the eternal life."

This is the Gospel of the Lord.

(Sit)

Homily

A brief homily based on the readings may be given.

Prayers of Intercession

LITANY

Minister: Let us offer our prayer through Jesus, who lived out the mystery of death and resurrection:

Enliven our hearts with a desire for heaven. To you we pray...

***All:* Lord, hear our prayer.**

Minister: Remember _____, who sought to follow your way of life. To you we pray...

***All:* Lord, hear our prayer.**

Minister: Enlighten us to see and accept the pattern of death and resurrection in our own lives. To you we pray...

***All:* Lord, hear our prayer.**

Minister: Increase our faith in your promise of new life. To you we pray...

***All:* Lord, hear our prayer.**

LORD'S PRAYER

Minister: Friends, we have the promise of new life. As heirs of this promise, let us pray confidently: **"Our Father..."**

CONCLUDING PRAYER

Minister: Let us pray.

God of life and death, we come to you believing that those who have died with your Son Jesus, are buried with Him in the sure hope of rising again. We pray in Jesus' name.

All: **Amen.**

It would be an appropriate time for members of the family or for friends to share their memories of the deceased. Likewise, it would be a suitable time to share a poem or a letter or to comment on a keepsake or simply to reminisce.

Concluding Rite

BLESSING OF THE BODY

The assembly is invited to bow their heads as the minister prays the final blessing:

Minister: We give you praise and we thank you, Father, for you formed our bodies from the dust of your beautiful creation, breathed into us your spirit, and gave us delight, that we can see, smell and hear, that we can taste and touch. We praise you, Lord, for _____, and we bless his/her body as we await the resurrection of the dead and the life of the world to come.

All: **Amen.**

A suitable song may conclude the service.

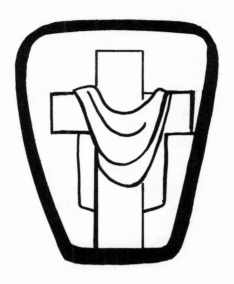

The Cross
Is Our Salvation

Symbol: Cross
Suggested Season: Lent or Ordinary Time

Introduction
Remain seated during the service till the Gospel.

OPENING SONG

WELCOME/INTRODUCTION OF THEME
The minister welcomes the family and friends informally and then proceeds with the service by <u>making the sign of the cross</u> and introducing the theme of the wake service (the minister can read the following introduction or comment on the symbol in his/her own words:)

Minister: The cross, which is folly to the world, is wisdom to the Christian. For it is by the cross that we have been saved from our sins. Jesus in John's Gospel proclaims that the Son of Man must be lifted up that all who believe may have eternal life in Him. The cross, forever a mystery, is the glorious sign of a Christian.

OPENING PRAYER

Minister: Father, we know that by the cross we have been saved. Through our baptism we entered into the mystery of the death and resurrection of Jesus. May the pain and suffering felt by family and friends become one with the cross and resurrection of Jesus. Amen.

The minister or one of the family may place the cross upon or near the casket.

Liturgy of the Word

PSALMS
The psalms may be recited by the gathering as a whole or alternately by sides 1 and 2.

● Psalm 77, 2-8 _____

All: Aloud to God I cry.

Side 1:
Aloud to God I cry:
    aloud to God, to hear me;
    on the day of my distress I seek the Lord.

Side 2:
By night my hands are stretched out without flagging;
    my soul refuses comfort.
When I remember God, I moan;
    when I ponder, my spirit grows faint.

Side 1:
You keep my eyes watchful;
  I am troubled and cannot speak.
I consider the days of old;
  the years long past I remember.
Side 2:
In the night I meditate in my heart;
  I ponder, and my spirit broods;
"Will the Lord reject forever
  and nevermore be favorable?"

● Psalm 116, 1-9 ———————————————————
All: Gracious is the Lord and just.
Side 1:
I love the LORD because he has heard
  my voice in supplication.
Because he has inclined his ear to me
  the day I called.
Side 2:
The cords of death encompassed me;
  the snares of the nether world seized upon me;
  I fell into distress and sorrow,
And I called upon the name of the LORD,
  "O LORD, save my life!"
Side 1:
Gracious is the LORD and just;
  yes, our God is merciful.
The LORD keeps the little ones;
  I was brought low, and he saved me.
Side 2:
Return, O my soul, to your tranquillity
  for the LORD has been good to you.
For he has freed my soul from death,
  my eyes from tears, my feet from stumbling
I shall walk before the LORD
  in the lands of the living.

SCRIPTURE READINGS

A member or friend of the family may present Reading A or B.

● Reading A ————————————————————

Reader: A reading from the prophet Isaiah (53, 2-5)

Like a sapling he grew up in front of us,
like a root in arid ground.
Without beauty, without majesty (we saw him),
no looks to attract our eyes;
a thing despised and rejected by men,
a man of sorrows and familiar with suffering,
a man to make people screen their faces;
he was despised and we took no account of him.

And yet ours were the sufferings he bore,
ours the sorrows he carried.
But we, we thought of him as someone punished,
struck by God, and brought low.
Yet he was pierced through for our faults,
crushed for our sins.

This is the Word of the Lord.

● Reading B ————————————————————

Reader: A reading from the letter of Paul to the Romans
(6, 3-4, 8-9)

You have been taught that when we were baptised in Christ
Jesus we were baptised in his death; in other words, when we
were baptised we went into the tomb with him and joined
him in death, so that as Christ was raised from the dead by the
Father's glory, we too might live a new life.

But we believe that having died with Christ we shall return
to life with him: Christ, as we know, having been raised from
the dead will never die again. Death has no power over him
any more. When he died, he died, once for all, to sin, so his

life now is life with God; and in that way, you too must consider yourselves to be dead to sin but alive for God in Christ Jesus.

This is the Word of the Lord.

Silence is suggested after the first reading. The Alleluia or another appropriate verse or song may introduce the Gospel.

● Gospel reading _____

(Stand)

Minister: A reading from the Gospel according to John (3, 13-17)

No one has gone up to heaven
except the one who came down from heaven,
the Son of Man who is in heaven;
and the Son of Man must be lifted up
as Moses lifted up the serpent in the desert,
so that everyone who believes may have eternal life in him.
Yes, God loved the world so much that he gave his only Son,
so that everyone who believes in him may not be lost
but may have eternal life.
For God sent his Son into the world
not to condemn the world,
but so that through him the world might be saved.

This is the Gospel of the Lord.

(Sit)

Homily
A brief homily based on the readings may be given.

Prayers of Intercession

LITANY

Minister: The Lord Jesus, out of his generous love, gave his life on the cross that we might be saved. Let us ask Him to deepen our faith and sustain us in bearing our daily crosses:

You showed us the way of suffering that leads to new life. Lord, in your mercy...

All: **Hear our prayer.**

Minister: You conquered death once and for all. By the power of your cross, protect ⟦Angelica⟧ and all those who hope in you. Lord, in your mercy...

All: **Hear our prayer.**

Minister: You entrusted your mother to the disciple John at the foot of the cross. Console us now in our time of sorrow and loss. Lord, in your mercy...

All: **Hear our prayer.**

Minister: You gave us the promise of resurrection to eternal life. Raise up ⟦Angelica⟧ to be with you for all eternity. Lord, in your mercy...

All: **Hear our prayer.**

Minister: You were forgiving of those who persecuted you. Show forgiveness to all the faithful departed. Lord, in your mercy...

All: **Hear our prayer.**

LORD'S PRAYER

Minister: We come with confidence to the Father through Jesus, our Savior, and pray: **"Our Father... "**

CONCLUDING PRAYER

Minister: Let us pray.

Father, Your Son, Jesus, by dying on the cross, has destroyed death and by rising has given us hope of eternal life. Strengthen us on our journey so that one day we will be reunited in heaven with those we have loved on this earth.

All: **Amen.**

It would be an appropriate time for the members of the family or for friends to share their memories of the deceased. Likewise it would be a suitable time to share a poem or letter or comment on a keepsake or simply to reminisce.

Concluding Rite

BLESSING OF THE BODY

The assembly is invited to bow their heads as the minister prays the final blessing:

Minister: We give you praise and we thank you, Father, for you formed our bodies from the dust of your beautiful creation, breathed into us your spirit, and gave us delight that we can see, smell and hear, that we can taste and touch. We praise you, Lord, for _____, whose body was a temple of your spirit, and we bless his/her body as we await the resurrection of the dead and the life of the world to come.

All: **Amen.**

A suitable song may conclude the service.

Birth Unto Hope

Symbol: Water
Suggested season: Easter or Ordinary Time

Introduction
Remain seated during the service till the Gospel.

OPENING SONG

WELCOME/INTRODUCTION OF THEME
The minister welcomes the family and friends informally and then proceeds with the service by making the sign of the cross and introducing the theme of the wake service (the minister can read the following introduction or comment of the symbol in his/her own words:)

Minister: Water in nature is a source of life, and Jesus used this life-giving symbol in the sacrament of Baptism. It is through this same sacrament that we become children of God and brothers and sisters in our family, the Church. Likewise, water is a reminder of the promise of eternal life. As we pour water into this bowl, we are reminded of Baptism.

The minister pours water from a pitcher into a bowl or the container used for the asperges and places the bowl near the casket.

OPENING PRAYER

Minister: Heavenly Father, source of all hope, we pour this water that reminds us of _____'s Baptism. Remember the promises you made to your son/daughter and welcome him/her into your heavenly dwelling place. We make this petition in Jesus' name. Amen.

Liturgy of the Word

PSALMS
The psalms may be recited by the gathering as a whole or alternately by sides 1 and 2.

● Psalm 42, 7-12 _____

All: Within me my soul is downcast.

Side 1:
Within me my soul is downcast;
   so will I remember you
From the land of the Jordan and of Hermon,
   from Mount Mizar.

Side 2:
Deep calls unto deep
   in the roar of your cataracts;
All your breakers and your billows
   pass over me.

Side 1:

By day the LORD bestows his grace,
 and at night I have his song,
 a prayer to my living God.

Side 2:

I sing to God, my rock:
 "Why do you forget me?
Why must I go about in mourning,
 with the enemy oppressing me?"

Side 1:

It crushes my bones that my foes mock me,
 as they say to me day after day, "Where is your God?"
Why are you so downcast, O my soul?
 Why do you sigh within me?

Side 2:

Hope in God! For I shall again be
 thanking him,
in the presence of my savior and my God.

● Psalm 25, 4-7 _____

All: In your kindness remember me.

Side 1:

Your ways, O LORD, make known to me;
 teach me your paths,
Guide me in your truth and teach me,
 for you are God my savior,
 and for you I wait all the day.

Side 2:

Remember that your compassion, O LORD,
 and your kindness are from of old.
The sins of my youth and my frailties remember not;
 in your kindness remember me,
 because of your goodness, O LORD.

SCRIPTURE READINGS
A member or friend of the family may present Reading A or B.

• Reading A ————————————————————————

Reader: A reading from the Book of Exodus (14, 21-31)

Moses stretched out his hand over the sea. Yahweh drove back the sea with a strong easterly wind all night, and he made dry land of the sea. The waters parted and the sons of Israel went on dry ground right into the sea, walls of water to right and to left of them. The Egyptians gave chase: after them they went, right into the sea, all Pharaoh's horses, his chariots, and his horsemen. In the morning watch, Yahweh looked down on the army of the Egyptians from the pillar of fire and of cloud, and threw the army into confusion. He so clogged their chariot wheels that they could scarcely make headway. "Let us flee from the Israelites," the Egyptians cried. "Yahweh is fighting for them against the Egyptians." "Stretch out your hand over the sea," Yahweh said to Moses, "that the waters may flow back on the Egyptians and their chariots and their horsemen." Moses stretched out his hand over the sea and, as day broke, the sea returned to its bed. The fleeing Egyptians marched right into it, and Yahweh overthrew the Egyptians in the very middle of the sea. The returning waters overwhelmed the chariots and the horsemen of Pharaoh's whole army, which had followed the Israelites into the sea; not a single one of them was left. But the sons of Israel had marched through the sea on dry ground, walls of water to right and to left of them. That day, Yahweh rescued Israel from the Egyptians, and Israel saw the Egyptians lying dead on the shore. Israel witnessed the great act that Yahweh had performed against the Egyptians, and the people venerated Yahweh; they put their faith in Yahweh and in Moses, his servant.

This is the Word of the Lord.

● Reading B _____

Reader: A reading from the first letter of Peter (1, 3-5)

Blessed be God the Father of our Lord Jesus Christ, who in his great mercy has given us a new birth as his sons, by raising Jesus Christ from the dead, so that we have a sure hope and the promise of an inheritance that can never be spoiled or soiled and never fade away, because it is being kept for you in the heavens. Through your faith, God's power will guard you until the salvation which has been prepared is revealed at the end of time.

This is the Word of the Lord.

Silence is suggested after the first reading. The Alleluia or another verse or song may introduce the Gospel.

● Gospel reading _____

(Stand)

Minister: A reading from the Gospel according to Matthew (28, 16-20)

Meanwhile the eleven disciples set out for Galilee, to the mountain where Jesus had arranged to meet them. When they saw him they fell down before him, though some hesitated. Jesus came up and spoke to them. He said, "All authority in heaven and on earth has been given to me. Go, therefore, make disciples of all the nations: baptize them in the name of Father and of the Son and of the Holy Spirit, and teach them to observe all the commands I gave you. And know that I am with you always: yes, to the end of time."

This is the Gospel of the Lord.

(Sit)

Homily

A brief homily based on the readings may be given.

Prayers of Intercession

LITANY

Minister: Our Heavenly Father has given us new birth as sons and daughters. And so we confidently pray:

Through the water of Baptism, the spirit of death is driven away and the Spirit of life appears. Through our Baptism, may we be filled with the Spirit of life for all eternity.

All: **Our hope is in the power of the Spirit.**

Minister: Through Baptism, we were united with Christ, dead and risen. May we who died to sin, rise someday with the triumphant Savior.

All: **Our hope is in the power of the Spirit.**

Minister: Through Baptism, _____ was born a child of God. May he/she be born again into the glorious life of eternity.

All: **Our hope is in the power of the Spirit.**

Minister: By the waters of Baptism, the power of sin was destroyed and God's grace abounds. May _____ experience the reward of a life lived in God's grace.

All: **Our hope is in the power of the Spirit.**

Minister: We have become co-heirs of heaven through Christ, our Savior. May Jesus give _____ the Kingdom he promised.

All: **Our hope is in the power of the Spirit.**

LORD'S PRAYER

Minister: Mindful of our inheritance as children of the Father, we say: **"Our Father..."**

CONCLUDING PRAYER

Minister: Lord, through the sacrament of Baptism, water has been given the power to destroy *and* give new life. May that power of water continue to destroy sin in our lives and give us new life till we are reunited with _____, who lives forever in your dwelling place.

All: **Amen.**

It would be an appropriate time for the members of the family or for friends to share their memories of the deceased. Likewise, it would be a suitable time to share a poem or letter or a keepsake or simply to reminisce.

Concluding Rite

BLESSING OF THE BODY
The family is invited to sprinkle the casket with the water poured in the basin. An aspergillum or an evergreen branch can be used. The assembly is invited to bow their heads as the minister prays the final blessing:

Minister: We give you praise and we thank you, Father, for you formed our bodies from the dust of your beautiful creation, breathed into us your spirit, and gave us delight that we can see, smell and hear, that we can taste and touch. We praise you, Lord, for _____, whose body was a temple of your spirit, and we bless his/her body as we await the resurrection of the dead and the life of the world to come.

All: **Amen.**

A suitable song may conclude the service.

Light That Conquers Darkness

Symbol: Candle *(A Christ candle may be used in the Easter season and an Advent candle during the Advent/Christmas season.)*
Suggested Season: Easter or Advent/Christmas

Introduction
Remain seated during the service till the Gospel.

OPENING SONG

WELCOME/INTRODUCTION OF THEME
The minister welcomes the family and friends informally and then proceeds with the service by making the sign of

the cross and introducing the theme of the wake service (minister can read the following introduction or comment on the symbol in his/her own words:)

Minister: The candle light is a reminder that Jesus came to conquer the darkness of sin and death. Luke writes in his Gospel that Jesus "who from on high will bring the rising Sun to visit us, to give light to those who live in darkness and the shadow of death..." (Luke 1, 78-79).

The minister or one of the family now lights a candle or candles near the casket.

OPENING PRAYER

Minister: Father, we awaited with longing for Jesus, the light of the world to appear. In His light, we have conquered sin. In the glorious light of the resurrection of Jesus, may _____, your servant, also conquer death. Amen.

The minister or a family member now lights the candle(s) near the casket.

Liturgy of the Word

PSALMS
The psalms may be recited by the gathering as a whole or alternately by sides 1 and 2.

● Psalm 42, 2-4, 6 _____

All: **My soul longs for you, O GOD.**

Side 1:
As the hind longs for the running waters,
 so my soul longs for you, O God.
Athirst is my soul for God, the living God.
 When shall I go and behold the face of GOD?

Side 2:
My tears are my food day and night,
 as they say to me day after day, "Where is your God?"

Side 1:
Why are you so downcast, O my soul?
 Why do you sigh within me?
Hope in God! For I shall again be
 thanking him,
in the presence of my savior and my God.

● Psalm 27, 1-4, 7-8, 13-14_____

All: The LORD is my light and my salvation.

Side 1:
The LORD is my light and my salvation;
 whom should I fear?
The LORD is my life's refuge;
 of whom should I be afraid?
One thing I ask of the LORD;
 this I seek:

Side 2:
To dwell in the house of the LORD
 all the days of my life.
That I may gaze on the loveliness of the LORD
 and contemplate his temple.

Side 1:
Hear, O LORD, the sound of my call:
 have pity on me, and answer me.
Of you my heart speaks; you my glance seeks;
 your presence, O LORD, I seek.

Side 2:
I believe that I shall see the bounty of the LORD
in the land of the living
Wait for the LORD with courage:
be stouthearted, and wait for the LORD.

SCRIPTURE READINGS
A member or friend of the family may present Reading A or B.
● Reading A _____

Reader: A reading from the prophet Isaiah (42, 6-7)
I, Yahweh, have called you to serve the cause of right;
I have taken you by the hand and formed you;
I have appointed you as a covenant of the people and light of
    the nations,
to open the eyes of the blind,
to free captives from prison,
and those who live in darkness from the dungeon.
This is the Word of the Lord.

● Reading B _____

Reader: A reading from the first letter of John (3, 1-3)
Think of the love that the Father has lavished on us,
by letting us be called God's children;
and that is what we are.
Because the world refused to acknowledge him,
therefore it does not acknowledge us.
My dear people, we are already the children of God
but what we are to be in the future has not yet been revealed;
all we know is, that when it is revealed
we shall be like him
because we shall see him as he really is.
Surely everyone who entertains this hope
must purify himself, must try to be as pure as Christ.
This is the Word of the Lord.
Silence is suggested after the first reading. An Alleluia or other
appropriate verse or song may introduce the Gospel.

● Gospel reading _____

(Stand)

Minister: A reading from the Gospel according to Matthew
(5, 14-16)

You are the light of the world. A city built on a hilltop cannot
be hidden. No one lights a lamp to put it under a tub; they
put it on the lampstand where it shines for everyone in the
house. In the same way your light must shine in the sight of
men, so that, seeing your good works they may give the praise
to your Father in heaven.

This is the Gospel of the Lord.

(SIT)

Homily
A brief homily based on the readings may be given.

Prayers of Intercession

LITANY   Stand

Minister: Trusting in the Father, Who through Jesus rescued
us from the darkness of sin and death, we pray:

God, Heavenly Father, You raised Jesus, Your Son, from the
grasp of death. May You also raise your adopted sons and
daughters. We pray...

All: **Be our light.**

Minister: In Baptism, _____ received the light of
Christ. Scatter the darkness of death and lead him/her to the
eternal light. We pray...

All: **Be our light.**

Minister: Christ, the light of the world, was present in the life of _____. May Christ also shine in our lives. We pray...

All: **Be our light.**

Minister: We are called to become a light in darkness in imitation of Jesus. Help us to follow You. We pray...

All: **Be our light.**

Minister: The family and friends of _____ seek the light and warmth of God's love and comfort. Heal the pain and dispel the darkness of their grief. We pray...

All: **Be our light.**

LORD'S PRAYER

Minister: Trusting in the revealing light of the Word of God, we now say, **"Our Father..."**

CONCLUDING PRAYER

Minister: Father of consoling light, You are with us in our journey through the valley of darkness. You guide us, gentle light, and lead us through the dangers of sin and death into the eternal glory of Your everlasting light.

All: **Amen.**

It would be an appropriate time for members of the family or for friends to share their memories of the deceased. Likewise, it would be a suitable time to share a poem or a letter or to comment on a keepsake or simply to reminisce.

Concluding Rite

BLESSING OF THE BODY
The assembly is invited to bow their heads as the minister prays the final blessing:

Minister: We give you praise and we thank you, Father, for you formed our bodies from the dust of your beautiful creation, breathed into us your spirit, and gave us delight that we can see, smell and hear, that we can taste and touch. We praise you, Lord, for _____, whose body was a temple of your spirit, and we bless his/her body as we await the resurrection of the dead and the life of the world to come.

All: **Amen.**

A suitable song may conclude the service.

Food for the Journey

Symbol: Bread and Wine
Suggested Season: Ordinary Time or Easter/Pentecost

Introduction

Remain seated during the service till the Gospel.

OPENING SONG

WELCOME/INTRODUCTION OF THEME
The minister welcomes the family and friends informally and then proceeds with the service by making the sign of the cross and introducing the theme of the wake service (the minister can read the following introduction or comment on the symbol in his/her own words:)

Minister: In the Eucharist we remember the death and resurrection of Jesus. Likewise in the Eucharist, Jesus gave Himself as spiritual nourishment for our life journey. Finally, the Eucharist, as spiritual food, is a foretaste of the Heavenly Banquet. Thus we look back to His death and resurrection, grow in His life through communion, and look forward to the eternal banquet.

The minister or one of the family now places a bottle of wine and loaf of bread on or near the casket.

OPENING PRAYER

Minister: Father, you so loved us that you gave Jesus to us as our daily food. Grant that _____, who ate often at the table of the Lord, may soon share in the Heavenly Banquet prepared for those who believe in Jesus, our Lord and Savior. Amen.

Liturgy of the Word

PSALMS

The psalms may be recited by the gathering as a whole or alternately by sides 1 and 2.

• Psalm 57, 2-4 _____

All: **In the shadow of your wings I take refuge.**

Side 1:

Have pity on me, O God; have pity on me,
for in you I take refuge.
In the shadow of your wings I take refuge,
till harm pass by.

Side 2:

I call to God the Most High
to God, my benefactor.
May he send from heaven and save me;
may he make those a reproach who trample upon me;
may God send his kindness and his faithfulness.

● Psalm 139, 1-6 ───────────────────────────

All: **O LORD, you have probed me and you know me.**

Side 1:
O LORD, you have probed me and you know me;
you know when I sit and when I stand;
you understand my thoughts from afar.

Side 2:
My journeys and my rest you scrutinize,
with all my ways you are familiar.
Even before a word is on my tongue,
behold, O LORD, you know the whole of it.

Side 1:
Behind me and before, you hem me in
and rest your hand upon me.
Such knowledge is too wonderful for me;
too lofty for me to attain.

SCRIPTURE READINGS
A member or friend of the family may present Reading A or B.
● Reading A ───────────────────────────

Reader: A reading from the first book of Kings (19, 1-8)

When Ahab told Jezebel all that Elijah had done, and how he had put all the prophets to the sword, Jezebel sent a messenger to Elijah to say, "May the gods do this to me and more, if by this time tomorrow I have not made your life like the life of one of them!" He was afraid and fled for his life. He came to Beersheba, a town of Judah, where he left his servant. He himself went on into the wilderness, a day's journey, and sitting under a furze bush wished he were dead. "Yahweh," he said, "I have had enough. Take my life; I am no better than my ancestors." Then he lay down and went to sleep. But an angel touched him and said, "Get up and eat." He looked around, and there at his head was a scone baked on hot stones, and a jar of water. He ate and drank and then lay down again.

But the angel of Yahweh came back a second time and touched him and said, "Get up and eat, or the journey will be too long for you." So he got up and ate and drank, and strengthened by that food he walked for forty days and forty nights until he reached Horeb, the mountain of God.

This is the Word of the Lord.

● Reading B _____

Reader: A reading from the first letter of Paul to the Corinthians (11, 23-26)

For this is what I received from the Lord, and in turn passed on to you: that on the same night that he was betrayed, the Lord Jesus took some bread, and thanked God for it and broke it, and he said, "This is my body, which is for you; do this as a memorial of me." In the same way he took the cup after supper, and said, "This cup is the new covenant in my blood. Whenever you drink it, do this as a memorial of me." Until the Lord comes, therefore every time you eat this bread and drink this cup, you are proclaiming his death.

This is the Word of the Lord.

Silence is suggested after the first reading. The Alleluia or another appropriate verse or song may introduce the Gospel.

● Gospel reading _____

(Stand)

Minister: A reading from the Gospel according to John (6, 51-59)

I am the living bread which has come down from heaven.
Anyone who eats this bread will live for ever;
and the bread that I shall give
is my flesh, for the life of the world."

Then the Jews started arguing with one another: "How can this man give us his flesh to eat?" they said. Jesus replied:

"I tell you most solemnly,
if you do not eat the flesh of the Son of Man
and drink his blood,
you will not have life in you.
Anyone who does eat my flesh and drink my blood
has eternal life,
and I shall raise him up on the last day.
For my flesh is real food
and my blood is real drink,
He who eats my flesh and drinks my blood
lives in me and I live in him.
As I, who am sent by the living Father,
myself draw life from the Father,
so whoever eats me will draw life from me.
This is the bread come down from heaven;
not like the bread our ancestors ate:
they are dead,
but anyone who eats this bread will live for ever."

This is the Gospel of the Lord.

(Sit)

Homily
A brief homily based on the reading may be given.

Prayers of Intercession

LITANY

Minister: Father, relying on your continuing generosity, we come before you with our petitions:

You called _____ to the banquet of Christ's body and blood. Now, call him/her to your heavenly banquet.

All: **You give us food and drink, Lord.**

Minister: You continue to provide us with nourishment for our hearts and souls. Never abandon us in our time of need.

All: **You give us food and drink, Lord.**

Minister: _____ hungered and thirsted for you during his/her life, O Lord; now satisfy his/her heart with that which gives life forever.

All: **You give us food and drink, Lord.**

Minister: You fed the prophet Elijah and made him strong in his journey. Feed us also and lead us on our sojourn.

All: **You give us food and drink, Lord.**

Minister: The Eucharist proclaims the death of Jesus until He comes in glory. Grant that all who believe in Jesus will also share in His glory.

All: **You give us food and drink, Lord.**

LORD'S PRAYER

Minister: Nourished by the Word of God and the Bread of Heaven, we have confidence to say: **"Our Father..."**

CONCLUDING PRAYER

Minister: Heavenly Father, You have provided your children nourishment for the heart and soul. You have strengthened us with food and drink in this life and given us the promise of a new life in your Kingdom where You reign forever and ever.

All: **Amen.**

It would be an appropriate time for members of the family or for friends to share their memories of the deceased. Likewise, it would be a suitable time to share a poem or letter or to comment on a keepsake or simply to reminisce.

Concluding Rite

BLESSING OF THE BODY

The assembly is invited to bow their heads as the minister prays the final blessing:

We give you praise and we thank you, Father, for you formed our bodies from the dust of your beautiful creation, breathed into us your spirit, and gave us delight that we can see, smell and hear, that we can taste and touch. We praise you, Lord, for _____, whose body was a temple of your spirit, and we bless his/her body as we await the resurrection of the dead and the life of the world to come.

All: **Amen.**

A suitable song may conclude the service.

In the Potter's Hands

Symbol: Earthen Vase
Suggested Season: Ordinary Time or Lent

Introduction
Remain seated during the service till the Gospel.

OPENING SONG

WELCOME/INTRODUCTION OF THEME
The minister welcomes the family and friends informally and then proceeds with the service by making the sign of the cross and introducing the theme of the wake service (the minister can read the following introduction or comment on the symbol in his/her own words:)

Minister: The Genesis story describes us as being fashioned from dirt or clay in the image of the Creator. God, as described by the Prophet Jeremiah, is a potter who lovingly fashions us, and when we are broken, refashions us. As the earthen vase (or pottery) is placed near the casket, we are reminded of our human origin, both fragile and precious.

The minister or one of the family now places an earthen vase or pottery near the casket.

OPENING PRAYER

Minister: Heavenly Creator, who fashioned us in our mother's womb and refashioned us throughout our journey of life, we entrust _____ into your Potter's hands. Give _____ new life as you welcome him/her into your heavenly mansion. We ask this through Christ, our Lord. Amen.

Liturgy of the Word

PSALMS
The psalms may be recited by the gathering as a whole or alternately by sides 1 and 2.

● Psalm 6, 1-5 _____

All: O, LORD, save my life.

Side 1:
O LORD, reprove me not in your anger,
  nor chastise me in your wrath.
Have pity on me, O LORD, for I am languishing;
  heal me, O LORD, for my body is in terror;

Side 2:
My soul, too, is utterly terrified;
  but you, O LORD, how long...?

Side 1:
Return, O LORD, save my life;
  rescue me because of your kindness.

● Psalm 9, 9-12 _____

All: The LORD is a stronghold for the oppressed.

Side 1:
He judges the world with justice;
  he governs the peoples with equity;
The LORD is a stronghold for the oppressed,
  a stronghold in times of distress.

Side 2:
They trust in you who cherish your name,
  for you forsake not those who seek you, O LORD.

Side 1:
Sing praise to the LORD enthroned in Zion;
  proclaim among the nations his deeds.

SCRIPTURE READINGS
A member or friend of the family may present Reading A or B.
● Reading A _____

Reader: A reading from the prophet Jeremiah (18, 1-7)

The word that was addressed to Jeremiah by Yahweh, "Get up and make your way down to the potter's house; there I shall let you hear what I have to say." So I went down to the potter's house; and there he was, working at the wheel. And whenever the vessel he was making came out wrong, as happens with the clay handled by potters, he would start afresh and work it into another vessel, as potters do. Then this word of Yahweh was addressed to me, "House of Israel, can not I do to you what this potter does? — it is Yahweh who speaks. Yes, as the clay is in the potter's hand, so you are in mine, House of Israel."

This is the Word of the Lord.

• Reading B

Readers: A reading from the second letter of Paul to the Corinthians (4, 5-12)

For it is not ourselves that we are preaching, but Christ Jesus as the Lord, and ourselves as your servants for Jesus' sake. It is the same God that said, "Let there be light shining out of darkness, who has shone in our minds to radiate the light of the knowledge of God's glory, the glory on the face of Christ.

We are only the earthenware jars that hold this treasure, to make it clear that such an overwhelming power comes from God and not from us. We are in difficulties on all sides, but never cornered; we see no answer to our problems, but never despair; we have been persecuted, but never deserted; knocked down, but never killed; always, wherever we may be, we carry with us in our body the death of Jesus, so that the life of Jesus, too, may always be seen in our body. Indeed, while we are still alive, we are consigned to our death every day, for the sake of Jesus, so that in our mortal flesh the life of Jesus, too, may be openly shown. So death is at work in us, but life in you.

This is the Word of the Lord.

Silence is suggested after the first reading. The Alleluia or another appropriate verse or song may introduce the Gospel.

• Gospel reading

(Stand)

Reader: A reading from the Gospel according to Luke (12, 22-32)

Then he said to his disciples, "That is why I am telling you not to worry about your life and what you are to eat, nor about your body and how you are to clothe it. For life means more than food, and the body more than clothing. Think of the ravens. They do not sow or reap; they have no storehouses and no barns; yet God feeds them. And how much more are you worth than the birds! Can any of you, for all his worrying, add a single cubit to his span of life? If the smallest things, therefore, are outside your control, why worry about the rest? Think of the flowers; they never have to spin or weave; yet, I assure you, not even Solomon in all his regalia was robed like one of these. Now if that is how God clothes the grass in the field which is there today and thrown into the furnace tomorrow, how much more will he look after you, you men of little faith! But you, you must not set your hearts on things to eat and things to drink; nor must you worry. It is the pagans of this world who set their hearts on all these things. Your Father well knows you need them. No; set your hearts on his kingdom, and these other things will be given you as well.

"There is no need to be afraid, little flock, for it has pleased your Father to give you the kingdom."

This is the Gospel of the Lord.

(Sit)

Homily
A brief homily based on the readings may be given.

Prayers of Intercession

LITANY

Minister: Lord, aware of your mercy, we come to you in simple faith:

Father, you gave Jesus new life and a glorious new body. In Jesus, You have promised us the same.

All: You are the Potter; we are the clay.

Minister: Lord, we all become fragile through aging and disease. Support us in our moments of brokenness and prepare us for new life.

All: **You are the Potter; we are the clay.**

Minister: Lord, you fashion us as unique sons and daughters of Yours. Continue in Your providence to refashion us again and again.

All: **You are the Potter; we are the clay.**

Minister: We acknowledge you, Heavenly Father, as the Potter who fashions our lives, even in the secrecy of the womb. Grant that you refashion the lowly body of _____ on the day of resurrection.

All: **You are the Potter; we are the clay.**

Minister: Lord, we have been broken often through sin. Through Your compassion, forgive and heal _____ of any brokenness through sin.

All: **You are the Potter; we are the clay.**

LORD'S PRAYER

Minister: Father, relying on your loving providence, we come to you in prayer: **"Our Father..."**

CONCLUDING PRAYER

Minister: Lord, in times of death, we are reminded of our fragile and mortal bodies. Yet with eyes of faith we also see our bodies as temples of the Spirit destined for eternal life. Grant that we may all someday be gathered together in glory through Christ our Lord.

All: **Amen.**

It would be an appropriate time for members of the family or friends to share their memories of the deceased. Likewise, it would be a suitable time to share a poem or letter or to comment on a keepsake or simply to reminisce.

Concluding Rite

BLESSING OF THE BODY

The assembly is invited to bow their heads as the minister prays the final blessing:

Minister: We give you praise and we thank you, Father, for you formed our bodies from the dust of your beautiful creation, breathed into us your spirit, and gave us delight that we can see, smell and hear, that we can taste and touch. We praise you, Lord, for _____, whose body was a temple of your spirit, and we bless his/her body as we await the resurrection of the dead and the life of the world to come.

All: **Amen.**

A suitable song may conclude the service.

The Life-Giving
Word of God

Symbol: Bible
Suggested Season: Ordinary Time or Easter/Pentecost

Introduction
Remain seated during the service till the Gospel.

OPENING SONG

WELCOME/INTRODUCTION OF THEME
The minister welcomes the family and friends informally and then proceeds with the service by making the sign of the cross and introducing the theme of the wake service (the minister can read the following or comment on the symbol in his/her own words:)

Minister: Our lives as Christians depend on the Word of God to nourish our faith and guide us in truth. It is the Bible that tells the great love story of God's pursuit of us, climaxing at Christmas in the gift of his Son, Jesus. The Word of God is used in every sacrament, beginning with Baptism. Finally, the Bible contains all the promises of God, thus feeding our hope for eternal life. Therefore, the Word of God consoles all of us in this time of grief.

OPENING PRAYER

Minister: God, our Father, we are the people of The Word. Your life-giving Word accompanies us throughout our lives, strengthening and consoling us especially in times of trial. Your Word reveals promises that give us hope. We place the Word of God upon (*or near*) the casket of _____ as a sign of your promise of Everlasting Life. Amen.

The minister or one of the family now places the Bible on or near the casket.

Liturgy of the Word

PSALMS
The psalms may be recited by the gathering as a whole or alternately by sides 1 and 2.

● Psalm 13,2-6 _____

All: How long, O LORD? Will you utterly forget me?

Side 1:
How long, O LORD? Will you utterly forget me?
How long will you hide your face from me?

Side 2:
How long shall I harbor sorrow in my soul,
   grief in my heart day after day?
How long will my enemy triumph over me?
   Look, answer me, O LORD, my God!

Side 1:
Give light to my eyes that I may not sleep in death
  lest my enemy say, "I have overcome him";
Lest my foes rejoice at my downfall
  though I trusted in your kindness.

Side 2:
Let my heart rejoice in your salvation;
  let me sing of the LORD, "He has been good to me."

● Psalm 23, 1-6 _____

All: Though I walk in the valley of darkness, I fear no evil,
for you are with me.

Side 1:
The LORD is my shepherd; I shall not want.
In verdant pastures he gives me repose;
Beside restful waters he leads me;
  he refreshes my soul.

Side 2:
He guides me in right paths
  for his name's sake.
Even though I walk in the dark valley
  I fear no evil; for you are at my side
With your rod and your staff that give me courage.

Side 1:
You spread the table before me
  in the sight of my foes;
You anoint my head with oil;
  my cup overflows.

Side 2:
Only goodness and kindness follow me
  all the days of my life;
And I shall dwell in the house of the LORD.

SCRIPTURE READINGS

A member or friend of the family may present Reading A or B.

• Reading A _____

Reader: A reading from the prophet Isaiah (55, 10-11)

Yes, as the rain and the snow come down from the heavens and do not return without watering the earth, making it yield and giving growth to provide seed for the sower and bread for the eating, so the word that goes from my mouth does not return to me empty, without carrying out my will and succeeding in what it was sent to do.

This is the Word of the Lord.

• Reading B _____

Reader: A reading from the letter to the Hebrews (4, 12-13)

The word of God is something alive and active: it cuts like any double-edged sword but more finely: it can slip through the place where the soul is divided from the spirit, or joints from the marrow; it can judge the secret emotions and thoughts. No created thing can hide from him; everything is uncovered and open to the eyes of the one to whom we must give account of ourselves.

This is the Word of the Lord.

Silence is suggested after the first reading. The Alleluia or another appropriate verse or song may introduce the Gospel reading.

• Gospel reading _____

(Stand)

Minister: A reading from the Gospel according to Matthew (7, 24-27)

"Therefore, everyone who listens to these words of mine and acts on them will be like a sensible man who built his house on a rock. Rain came down, floods rose, gales blew and hurled themselves against that house, and it did not fall: it was founded on rock. But everyone who listens to these words of mine and does not act on them will be like a stupid man who built his house on sand. Rain came down, floods rose, gales blew and struck that house, and it fell; and what a fall it had!"

This is the Gospel of the Lord.

(Sit)

Homily
A brief homily based on the readings may be given.

Prayers of Intercession

LITANY

Minister: God, our Father, mindful that You are ever true to Your Word, we bring our needs before You in simple trust:

Word of God, comfort us in our sorrow. Lord, have mercy.

All: Lord, have mercy.

Minister: Source of life, grant eternal life to your servant _____. Lord, have mercy.

All: Lord, have mercy.

Minister: Promise of the Ages, renew our faith in your Word. Lord, have mercy.

All: Lord, have mercy.

Minister: Hope of those who trust in You, guide us on our way. Lord, have mercy.

All: Lord, have mercy.

Minister: Redeemer of your people, show mercy to
_____, who believed in you. Lord, have mercy.

All: **Lord, have mercy.**

Minister: Healer of the sorrowing, open our hearts to your
life-giving Word. Lord, have mercy.

All: **Lord, have mercy.**

LORD'S PRAYER
Minister: Trusting in that life-giving Word, which reveals
God as Father, let us pray: **"Our Father..."**

CONCLUDING PRAYER
Minister: Father, you sent your Son, Jesus, as the living
Word. By His death we are strengthened and by His
resurrection we are given hope. Make our faith strong
through Christ our Lord. Amen.

*It would be an appropriate time for members of the family or for
friends to share their memories of the deceased. Likewise, it would
be a suitable time to share a poem or letter or to comment on a
keepsake or simply to reminisce.*

Concluding Rite

BLESSING OF THE BODY
*The assembly is invited to bow their heads as the minister prays the
final blessing:*

Minister: We give you praise and we thank you, Father, for
you formed our bodies from the dust of your beautiful
creation, breathed into us your spirit, and gave us delight that
we can see, smell and hear, that we can taste and touch. We
praise you, Lord, for _____, whose body was a temple
of your Spirit, and we bless his/her body as we await the
resurrection of the dead and the life of the world to come.

All: **Amen.**

A suitable song may conclude the service.

Appendix 1

Alternate Scripture Readings

"Like Incense Before You": Exodus 30, 1-2a, 7-8; 40, 1-5; Numbers 16, 16-18; Leviticus 2, 1-3, 5-6; Luke 1, 8-13.

"God of Faithfulness": Jeremiah 17, 7-9; Zechariah 8, 1-8; Isaiah 38, 19-20; Romans 15, 4-9; I Corinthians 1, 3-9; I Timothy 6, 11-16; John 5, 19-21; John 14, 16-21.

"Life Is Changed, Not Ended": Genesis 1, 11-12; Daniel 12, 1-3; Romans 15, 5-10; I Corinthians 15, 35-38, 42-44; Titus 2, 11-14; I Thessalonians 4, 14-18; I John 3, 1-3; John 12, 23-25; John 11, 17-27.

"The Cross Is Our Salvation": I Corinthians 1, 18-25; I Corinthians 15, 54-58; 2 Corinthians 4, 14; 5, 1; I John 5, 4-6; John 19, 17-18, 25-39; Mark 8, 34-37.

"Birth Unto Hope": Ezekiel 47, 1-3, 5-6; Genesis 2, 4a-11; I Peter 3, 18-21; Acts 10, 44-48; Hebrews 10, 19-24; Revelation 22, 1-2, 17; John 7, 37-39; John 3, 1-5.

"The Light That Conquers Darkness": Isaiah 60, 1-5; Proverbs 4, 10-13, 18-19; I Peter 2, 9-10; Revelation 22, 1-5; Luke 2, 25-32; Luke 11, 33-36.

"Food for the Journey": Isaiah 25, 6-9; Deuteronomy 8, 1-3; Nehemiah 9, 14-15; I Corinthians 5, 6-8; Matthew 26, 26-30; John 6, 32-35.

"In the Potter's Hands": Genesis 2, 4-7; Isaiah 64, 2-3, 6-7; II Timothy 2, 20-21; Romans 9, 19-21; II Corinthians 5, 1-10; I Corinthians 15, 47-49; Luke 15, 11-24.

"The Life-Giving Word of God": Ezekiel 3, 1-4; I Thessalonians 1, 5-8; Romans 10, 14-17; Hebrews 13, 7-8; I Peter 1, 22-23; Ephesians 1, 11-14; Matthew 13, 3-9; John 14, 23-24.

Appendix 2

Music for Wake Services

A Banquet Is Prepared (John Kavanaugh, S.J.)
Abba! Father! (Carey Landry)
All I Ask of You (Gregory Norbet, O.S.B.)
All My Days (Dan Schutte, S.J.)
All That We Have (Gary Ault)
Amazing Grace (Traditional)
Baptism Prayer (Tim Schoenbachler)
Beatitudes (Darryl Ducote)
Be Not Afraid (Bob Dufford, S.J.)
Be With Me Lord (Marty Haugen)
Be With Me Lord (Michael Joncas)
Blessing (James Marchionda, O.P.)
Blest Be the Lord (Dan Schutte, S.J.)
Come, My Way, My Truth, My Life (Ralph Vaughan Williams)
Come, Return to the Lord (Carey Landry)
Come to Me, All Who Are Weary (Dan Schutte, S.J.)
Come to the Water (John Foley, S.J.)
Crown Him with Many Crowns (George J. Elvey)
Cry of the Poor, The (John Foley, S.J.)
Dance in the Darkness (Carey Landry)
Day Is Done (James Dominick Quinn, S.J.)
Dwelling Place (John Foley, S.J.)
Do Not Fear to Hope (Rory Cooney)
Earthen Vessel (John Foley, S.J.)
Eye Has Not Seen (Marty Haugen)
Faithful Family (Rory Cooney)
For All the Saints (Ralph Vaughan Williams)
For Us to Live (Gregory Norbet, O.S.B.)
For You Are My God (John Foley, S.J.)
Gentle Shepherd (Fr. Tobias Colgan, O.S.B.)
Goodness of God, The (Gregory Norbet, O.S.B.)
How Great Thou Art (Stuart Hine)
How Lovely Is Your Dwelling Place (Michael Joncas)

I Am the Bread of Life (Suzanne Toolan)
I Am the Resurrection (Jim Anderson)
If God Is for Us (John Foley, S.J.)
I Have Loved You (Michael Joncas)
I Lift Up My Soul (Jim Manion)
I Long for You (Mike Balhoff, Gary Daigle, Darryl Ducote)
I Rejoiced (John Foley, S.J.)
Isaiah 49 (Carey Landry)
I, the Lord (Tom Kendzia)
Just a Closer Walk (Unknown)
Keep in Mind (Lucien Deiss)
Like a Shepherd (Bob Dufford, S.J.)
Living Hope, A (Michael W. Jones)
Lord Is Kind, The (Rory Cooney)
Lord Is My Shepherd, The (Joe Wise)
Lord Is Near, The (Michael Joncas)
Lord, to Whom Shall We Go (Michael Joncas)
Lord's Prayer, The (Gregory Norbet, O.S.B.)
My Friends, I Bless You (Gregory Norbet, O.S.B.)
My Prayers Rise Like Incense (Michael Joncas)
My Soul Is Longing for Your Peace (Lucien Deiss)
O Come, O Come Emmanuel (adapted by Thomas Helmore)
On Eagle's Wings (Michael Joncas)
Only a Shadow (Carey Landry)
Only In God (John Michael Talbot)
Only in God (John Foley, S.J.)
Peace Is Flowing Like a River (Carey Landry)
Peace of the Lord, The (Gary Ault)
Peace Prayer (John Foley, S.J.)
Praise the Lord My Soul (John Foley, S.J.)
Praised Be the Father (Mike Balhoff, Darryl Ducote, Gary Daigle)
Prayer of St. Francis (Sebastian Temple)
Psalm of the Good Shepherd (Carey Landry)
Psalm 33; Song of the Chosen (Rory Cooney)
Remember Your Love (Gary Daigle, Darryl Ducote)
Shelter Me, O God (Bob Hurd)
Sing a New Song (Dan Schutte, S.J.)
Sing to the Mountains (Bob Dufford, S.J.)
Song of Baptism (Carey Landry)
Song of Thanksgiving (Darryl Ducote)
Sun Is Rising, The (Gregory Norbet, O.S.B.)
This Alone (Tim Manion)

Turn to Me (John Foley, S.J.)
Unless a Grain of Wheat (Bob Hurd)
We Are the Light of the World (Jean Anthony Greif)
We Have Been Told (David Haas)
We Remember (Marty Haugen)
We Stand In Need (Michael B. Lynch)
We Walk by Faith (Marty Haugen)
Wherever You Go (Gregory Norbet, O.S.B.)
With the Lord (Michael Joncas)
With the Lord, There Is Mercy (Marty Haugen)
Yahweh Is My Shepherd (Millie Rieth)
Yahweh, the Faithful One (Dan Schutte, S.J.)
You Alone (Rory Cooney)
You Are Near (Dan Schutte, S.J.)

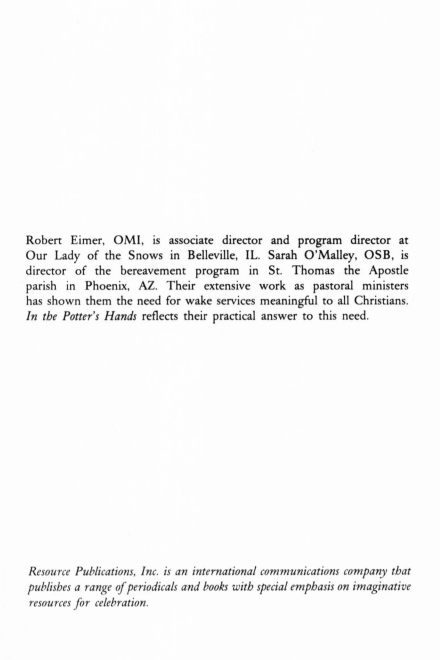

Robert Eimer, OMI, is associate director and program director at Our Lady of the Snows in Belleville, IL. Sarah O'Malley, OSB, is director of the bereavement program in St. Thomas the Apostle parish in Phoenix, AZ. Their extensive work as pastoral ministers has shown them the need for wake services meaningful to all Christians. *In the Potter's Hands* reflects their practical answer to this need.

Resource Publications, Inc. is an international communications company that publishes a range of periodicals and books with special emphasis on imaginative resources for celebration.